Original title:
The Sea's Hidden Heart

Copyright © 2025 Creative Arts Management OÜ
All rights reserved.

Author: Wyatt Kensington
ISBN HARDBACK: 978-1-80587-306-8
ISBN PAPERBACK: 978-1-80587-776-9

Underwater Dreams

Bubbles rise like silly balloons,
Fish dance to their quirky tunes,
A crab in a tux, all dressed to impress,
Must be late for the ocean's big fest.

Octopuses juggle with bubbles of goo,
Floors made of sand where the starfishes glue,
Seahorses prance like they're in a parade,
While turtles groove in their shell-made charades.

Fluid Poetry in Motion

Waves whisper secrets to the clam,
As jellyfish float, doing the jam,
Anemones pulling their friends in tight,
While seaweed twirls, feeling delight.

Dolphins in bow ties, smiling with glee,
Talk strategies for the next big spree,
Crabs take bets on the best slip and slide,
As fish set up a carnival tide.

Echoes of Abandoned Shores

Shells on the beach, they gossip and wink,
About a whale who forgot how to sink,
A seagull's joke brings the sand-dwellers cheer,
As they gather around for the annual leer.

Starfish are busy painting their toes,
While clams play charades with a chorus of woes,
Seashells giggle under the sun's glare,
The jokes on the tide, but who really cares?

Enigma of the Tidal Flow

A wave that trips on its own two feet,
Carrying tales of a fish's retreat,
Crabs rolling dice on the sandy old floor,
Betting who'll swim to the dolphin's shore.

Mermaids knitting seaweed for fun,
Yarn that sparkles like bright morning sun,
Fish in sombreros, salsa on the side,
Ride the swells of laughter, a buoyant tide.

The Silent Song of Sirens

In waters deep, a chorus hums,
With fishy flutes and seaweed drums.
A crab taps beat on a sailor's toe,
While dolphins dance in a wavy show.

The mermaids giggle, tails in a twist,
Their secret concerts rarely missed.
But sailors hear just squeaks and croaks,
As they debate all their ocean jokes.

Beneath the Veil of Neptune

A jellyfish winks, all dressed in lace,
While octopus pulls a funny face.
He juggles shells, with flair and grace,
But trips and lands in a perfect place.

Crabs in tuxedos, they're here to dance,
Slipping and sliding, they take a chance.
A tidepool bash, their kind of spree,
Reminds us all: be silly, be free!

Ocean's Veins of Mystery

In coral caves, the clowns reside,
With sea anemones as their guide.
They throw a party on a whim,
With disco lights and fish that swim.

A sea turtle sports a tie so bright,
While starfish play cards deep in the night.
The gossip flows through the ocean floor,
Of treasures lost and legends more.

Shadows in the Blue

A whale swims by, a graceful sight,
With curious fish that leap in fright.
They hide in kelp, avoid the stare,
Of shadows dancing without a care.

The anglerfish, with its cheeky grin,
Lures in friends, who might just swim.
They chat about sunsets and moonlit charms,
In their own quirky, underwater farms.

Lurking Tides of Emotion

Bubbles rise with giggles loud,
As fish in bowties swim quite proud.
Octopus juggles shells with flair,
While seahorses tease without a care.

Crabs throw a party, claws in air,
Dancing sideways without a scare.
The mermaids laugh, their hair a mess,
Creating chaos, causing stress.

Treasures in the Abyss

A pirate's hat floats by, oh dear,
It smells like treasure, or maybe beer?
With snails in suits, they stake their claim,
In a world where sea slugs play the game.

Gold doubloons reflect the sun,
But here, they're just for silly fun.
The clams are plotting, what a mix,
Their secret stash of old, lost tricks.

Murmurs of the Blue

The waves whisper jokes, so absurd,
About fish who think they're flightless birds.
A dolphin slips, the crowd erupts,
As gulls retell tales, and laughter erupts.

Starfish recite poetry with glee,
While playing chess with a wise old sea.
The ocean giggles, deep and wide,
With secrets laughing beneath the tide.

Silent Depths of Desire

Anemones blush when they meet the sun,
While turtles attempt a somersault run.
Seahorses swoon, love's awkward dance,
In swirling currents, they take a chance.

Whales serenade with tunes quite silly,
Echoes giggle, making us silly.
Love notes trapped in bubbles float,
Just don't ask the jellyfish to gloat.

Fishscale Fantasies

In waters deep, folks often guess,
Fish wear shoes, what a stylish mess!
With fins that twirl and scales that gleam,
They dance like stars in a fishy dream.

Bubbles rise like giggles, oh so bright,
A crab with a top hat, what a sight!
Seahorses race on invisible tracks,
While jellyfish bounce with their snappy slacks.

Forgotten Ruins of the Tide

Amidst the shells, there's a chair so grand,
Built by clams, just as they planned.
The fish gossip in hushed, silly tones,
About a sea queen made of bones!

Her crown's made of seaweed, a lovely weave,
While the octopus stirs a big bowl of peas.
Each wave whispers secrets of times past,
As sea turtles giggle, a sight unsurpassed.

Pearl-Guarded Secrets

A clam claims pearls, but they're just old coins,
He thinks he's rich, what a funny choice!
With whispers of treasure, he's full of pride,
But gulls just laugh, they've seen him slide.

A mermaid swims, who's a bit of a tease,
Trading fish tales like old, floppy keys.
With dolphins snorting, they make quite the show,
Even the seaweed sways to and fro.

Dances in the Foam

The waves do jiggles, jump, and sway,
While crabs hold a ball, come join the play!
Starfish spin in a graceful twirl,
As sea cucumbers join with a whirl.

The seagulls squawk a comical tune,
While fish parade under the bright full moon.
In foam, they leap with a splashy delight,
Where laughter echoes through the night!

Heartbeats Beneath Coral

In a realm where mermaids dance,
Fish trade gossip at a glance.
Octopuses play poker quite rude,
While clams throw parties with lots of food.

The sea turtles wear tiny hats,
Jellyfish boogie, how about that?
Crabs in tuxedos, counting their bucks,
And starfish give advice - only bad luck!

Eels twist like dancers untrained,
While seahorses giggle, at nothing they feigned.
The treasure chest has a ticklish lid,
Where sea cucumbers hide and bid.

But beware the seagulls, they steal the scene,
And laugh at fish jokes that are quite mean.
When the tide comes in, it's all a game,
In the deep below, it's never the same.

Shadows of Forgotten Ships

Ghostly ships drift with a creak,
Lost to time, but not to sneak peaks.
The captain's ghost has a humor so dry,
Stealing poor sailors' bread as they sigh.

Cannons stand like grumpy old men,
Recounting glory days now and then.
The compass spins like it's lost its way,
While barnacles sing, 'Come out to play!'

A parrot squawks, 'Polly wants a treat!'
But glares at fishes, 'You can't be discreet!'
The ship's wheel spins, oh what a knuckle,
As mermaids come by to share some chuckle.

Hidden treasures planned a prank,
To make gulls wear hats, oh how they'll tank!
In the depths, the laughter's still loud,
Amongst shadows where the fish are proud.

The Call of the Sirens

Sorry mate, we sing for fun,
Not to lure you, oh no, not one!
With voices sweet and jokes that slay,
We charm the brave to join our play.

Shiny scales that gleam like sun,
As they serenade, the mullet run.
They tell tall tales of fishy lore,
While seahorses listen, desperate for more.

With waves as their stage, they strut and leap,
While crabs in the crowd, their secrets keep.
A bubble-blower makes the audience gasp,
With bursts so funny, they can't help but clasp.

Yet when sailors heed the call too true,
They find seaweed stashed in the loo!
Sirens just giggle, and dance on rocks,
Trading tales with the watchful flocks.

Secrets of the Deep Blue

Deep below where the fish wear ties,
Eels catch gossip, oh what a surprise!
With secrets traded in bubbles and winks,
And every fish laughing as no one thinks.

The starfish map out a game of tag,
In underwater hideouts, never a brag.
Sea turtles shuffle, their age unclear,
With stories from days when the sea was near.

Clownfish jest, with colors bright,
Telling dad jokes that feel just right.
With fillings of laughter and giggles galore,
The ocean's pulse, you just can't ignore.

In currents swift, joy's the intent,
And every wave is a good-humor's scent.
So swim along with the quirkiest crew,
There's never a dull wave in the blue!

Chasing Shadows in the Deep

In the depths where fish wear shades,
A crab moonwalks, and laughter cascades.
Jellyfish dance in a glowing rave,
While seaweed whispers, 'Hey, be brave!'

Hermit crabs hold talent shows,
Competing in funny shell-shaped clothes.
They strut their stuff, a sight so rare,
While starfish cheer without a care.

Bubble-blowing dolphins play tag,
With octopuses waving their flag.
Every splash brings a giggling swell,
As sea creatures giggle, 'Aqua's swell!'

So dive on down, and you'll soon find,
The ocean's laughter is one of a kind.
With every wave and jolly cheer,
You'll leave the deep with a splash of cheer!

Coral Cradles of Lost Hope

Corals weave tales, colorful and bright,
Of a fish who got stuck in a nightlight.
They giggle at snails with their slow, sad pace,
While clams come out to show their new face.

Once a turtle couldn't quite glide,
Tangled in treasures he tried to hide.
He cracked a pun, 'I'm not lost at sea,
Just exploring the world's quirk, can't you see?'

A mermaid sings of socks and lost shoes,
Her fishy friends hum the latest news.
'Have you seen my shiny brush?' she pleads,
While anemones dodge jokes with glee indeed.

So next time you think hope's out of reach,
Remember the tales that corals can teach.
In this world, laughter's a guiding star,
Even in currents, you'll go far!

Beneath the Surface: A Lullaby

In bubble beds where starfish snore,
The ocean rocks them with tales galore.
Clownfish giggle, sharing sweet dreams,
As shrimps tap their shells to make funny themes.

A sleepy whale hums a soft tune,
'This bed of kelp feels just like a boon.'
While tiny krill take a sleepy ride,
On narwhal backs, a lively slide.

The ocean floor holds a slumbering jive,
Where sea cucumbers dance to stay alive.
With laughter echoing in waves above,
Sweet dreams linger, wrapped in love.

So drift on down with a giggle or snore,
Beneath the waves, there's fun to explore.
Every ripple brings a lullaby sweet,
With joy in the depths where sea critters meet!

Crashing Waves and Silent Souls

Waves crash in a hiccuping spree,
As seagulls squawk, 'That's quite a fee!'
A fish with goggles swims with flair,
While sea lions giggle, 'Catch that air!'

Barnacles form a rock band, oh dear,
Playing tunes that only crabs can hear.
With clapping fins and shells that shine,
Their music sways in salty brine.

An octopus juggles with a great flair,
'How many balls? I think, oh, beware!'
But just two land on jellyfish heads,
'It's fine,' they giggle, 'We sleep in beds.'

So when you feel a splash of surprise,
Remember the laughter beneath sunny skies.
In crashing waves, the joy can unfold,
With funny tales of misfits bold!

Heartbeat of the Abyssal Realm

Down in the deep where the fishes sing,
The octopus dances, it's quite the fling.
With a tentacle wave, it steals your snack,
And shimmies away, it's no skillful act.

The shrimp throw a bash, the crabs join in,
With a side of plankton, they all chime in.
The anglerfish smirks with its glowing lure,
Appearing like good bait, but who can be sure?

Whales on their phones share the latest memes,
As bubbles float up like colorful dreams.
Each splash tells a tale, bursting with cheer,
Running a carnival down in the sphere.

So dive down below where the laughter flows,
With seaweed wigs and the best of shows.
The depths may be dark, but the humor is bright,
In this underwater circus, it's pure delight.

Veiled Shores of Forgotten Lore

At the water's edge, the gulls bark and tease,
With secrets of sailors among the sea breeze.
A treasure chest waits with a pirate's grin,
But open it up and watch the fish swim in!

With tales of old pirates who lost their gold,
The legends get richer as the stories unfold.
A clam wearing glasses recites an old song,
While jellyfish dance, and nothing feels wrong.

Sandcastles rise with the tides, they say,
Only to tumble and wash them away.
Seagulls applaud, what a sight to behold,
As they steal your sandwich, so brash, so bold!

Yet laughter escapes from the salty waves,
In this quirky realm where the ocean misbehaves.
The shores may be veiled, but the jokes stay clear,
Join the tide's humor, and forget all your fear.

The Guardian of Sunken Paths

An elder turtle with a beard so grand,
Guards tales of the ocean, wise and unplanned.
With a wink and a nod, it points to the sand,
To treasures forgotten in the waves, oh so bland.

"Watch out for dolphins, they'd steal your hat!"
It chuckles softly, and how we all spat!
They leap and they dance, so slick and so sly,
Only to nudge me with a mischievous eye.

Starfish hold meetings, discussing their ways,
While sea cucumbers sleep through the days.
"Life's just a current!" they declare with a laugh,
As they float around, showing off their craft.

So heed well the guardian, wise in its art,
For the ocean holds humor within its great heart.
Every ripple and wave can giggle and prance,
In this realm of surprises, come join in the dance!

Caves of Whispering Waters

In caves where the water drips with a plop,
Fish gather around for a laugh and a flop.
Echoes of giggles bounce off the wall,
As seaweed sways, echoing their call.

"Did you hear the one about the crab and the beer?"
One goldfish gaffaws, it's that time of year!
Dancing in circles, the trout join the fun,
With bubbles of laughter, all under the sun.

The otters play games in the smooth, cool tide,
While snappy old lobsters refuse to collide.
"Move aside, you crustaceans, give us some room,
We're churning out jokes for the fish at high noon!"

So slide down the currents, let laughter arise,
Through caves of whispers, where humor defies.
The tides might be rough, but joy finds a way,
In the hugs of the waters, we play all day.

The Ocean's Enigmatic Pulse

Bubbles rise and giggle loud,
Fishes dance, a wiggly crowd.
Crabs wear hats, they strut in line,
A party under waves, so divine.

Jellyfish float like balloons,
Tickling turtles with silly tunes.
Seaweed sways in rhythmic play,
As starfish cheer for a holiday!

Octopuses juggle with flair,
While mermaids tease with shiny hair.
A clam sings opera, proud and bright,
As dolphins laugh throughout the night.

Tides do the cha-cha, waves do the twist,
A treasure chest joins the dance, can't resist!
In this underwater shindig, take part,
Join the laughter—it's a watery art!

Waves Whisper Secrets

The waves chuckle, a splashy cheer,
They tell tales that only fish hear.
A crab's wearing shoes, oh what a sight,
Stepping on seaweed, trying to be bright.

A whale sings low, a jolly tune,
While sea turtles spin like a cartoon.
Barnacles clapped on a soggy log,
With jokes that could make a clam full of smog.

Sea stars gossip, sharing the gossip,
While a playful dolphin does a flip-flop.
Anemones dance to a rhythm unknown,
In a coral club that's all their own.

The shoreline hears, the gulls squawk back,
As waves whisper secrets they never lack.
With giggles and splashes, the water laughs,
Creating a world of silliness that quaffs!

Beneath the Ocean's Veil

In depths where jellybeans abound,
The clams wear glasses, oh so profound!
A fish in a tux makes a dapper show,
Sipping on seafoam, how d'you do, hello!

A turtle spins tales of a shipwrecked purse,
While barnacles grumble, it could be worse.
Mermaids pull pranks, with glittery tricks,
Which lead to calamities, giggles and flicks.

Bubbles dance like party balloons,
As a sea sponge dons ridiculous looms.
A crab's got jokes, his punchlines are jokes,
Feeding the fishes with chuckles and pokes.

An octopus plays the drum with flair,
Keeping the beat while fishes stop and stare.
With laughter and glee, beneath the bright blue,
Are underwater shenanigans, all for the crew!

Echoes of the Deep

Echoes swirl in the cobalt blue,
Where fish form a conga line, yes it's true!
Anemones giggle, tickling tiny toes,
While crabs set up shop for the lost things they chose.

A whale gives a wink, with a twinkle in eye,
As clownfish swim by with a goofy sigh.
The seashells compose a memorable tune,
Spinning the tales of the ocean's cartoon.

Turtles toast with kelp for a treat,
As seahorses dance to their fancy beat.
A ray plays the harp, it's a silken affair,
While shrimp in tuxedos bow with flair.

So gather around, let the waves play their part,
In this symphonic haunt filled with laughter and art.
Trust the ocean's echoes, for joy they bestow,
In the depths of the waters, where silliness flows!

Tidal Echoes and Forgotten Tales

In the depths where fish do dance,
Crabs in tuxedos take a chance.
A clam may sing, though not so well,
Its rhymes as lost as stories tell.

Octopuses throw wild parties,
While lazy sharks just nap and snore.
Barnacles are gluey mates,
Crafting tales of ocean's fates.

Seahorses wear cute bow ties,
Flipping tales of seaweed pies.
They boast of bubbles, smooth and round,
Their humor often knows no bounds.

Remember, shells can tell a joke,
While jellyfish just float and poke.
In currents swift, the giggles swell,
For ocean life is grand, quite swell!

Celestial Mariner's Secrets

A starfish claims it saw a moon,
That danced with waves and hummed a tune.
But fish just giggle at the sight,
And wave their tails in pure delight.

Whales wear crowns of seaweed green,
As if they were the ocean's queen.
With bubble rings and playful splashes,
They tease the dolphins in quick dashes.

Shrimp throw parties in a whirl,
While seagulls dive and give a twirl.
Each fish tells tales of deeper tricks,
Of pirate ghosts and fancy flicks.

Coral reefs play hide and seek,
With creatures bold and some quite meek.
In the depths, where laughter grows,
Secrets hide beneath the flows.

The Subaquatic Symphony

Bubbles pop in a rhythmic beat,
As fishes gather for a treat.
Anemones sway with glee and flair,
While sea snails try to dance with care.

A band of crabs performs a show,
With marching steps and flashy toe.
The flounder jigs, the puffer sways,
Each note brings giggles, loud displays.

Starry skies take the ocean stage,
As whales recite a watery page.
Their deep voices echo, robust and bright,
In this silent humor-filled light.

The clowns of the reef, colorful and bold,
Share laughs and stories through the cold.
In the ocean's laugh, we all take part,
In playful notes from the music's heart.

A Realm Beneath the Foamy Crest

Among the waves where sunsets blend,
Hydras chill and jellyfish send.
They wear the crowns of seaweed flair,
Who knew deep down it's fun down there?

Nudibranchs are the fashion foes,
Playing tricks with each color that glows.
They prance and preen, no time to rest,
While crabs pass out "Oceans Best" tests.

Seashells clink like wind chimes sweet,
As starry knights prepare to meet.
Sardines squabble, cramming tight,
In a dazzling fishy pillow fight.

Beneath the crest, where laughter's free,
The fish ballet in gleeful spree.
Together we find the joy that's true,
In the deep's embrace, for me and you!

The Enigma of Drowned Suns

Under waves, lost stars they say,
Fish chuckle at suns that lost their way.
Crabs host parties near the kelp grove,
Jellyfish twirl in a plus-size robe.

Seashells gossip about the moon's face,
Seagulls swoop in with a cheeky grace.
The currents giggle and play hide and seek,
While dolphins prank, making humans squeak.

Barnacles dance in their crusty wear,
Claiming a rock like a millionaire.
Octopus painters with tentacles wide,
Splash colors of chaos full of pride.

Each tide brings tales from depths unknown,
Mermaids scandalize with laughter and groan.
Treasure lies buried beneath the foam,
Where no one bothered to make their home.

Reflections in a Salted Mirror

Waves shimmer like cheese on a Sunday toast,
The sun makes the sea look like a strange host.
Starfish argue about who's the best,
While crabs ignore them, just taking a rest.

Seagulls strut like they've won a prize,
Throwing shade with their judgmental eyes.
A whale hums jokes in a deep, deep low,
While turtles giggle, just taking it slow.

Shells hold secrets, if they could just speak,
Of pirate parties and games that they sneak.
A fish wears a hat made of seaweed spray,
Proclaiming it's fashionable, come what may.

In this salty mirror, humor can flow,
With every swell, more laughter will grow.
As dolphins flip like they're on a spree,
Who knew the ocean could be so funny?

The Depths' Quiet Confession

Bubbles rise with a whispering tale,
Of lost flip-flops on a whimsical trail.
Fish gossip softly, like they've seen the light,
As they dodge nets in their daring flight.

Octopuses swap hats in a crazy style,
As sea cucumbers sit back and smile.
The rocks conspire, with moss as their guide,
While shrimp do impressions with joyful pride.

A coral reef teases the passing tide,
Daring it to change which way it will glide.
Starfish claim to know all the best spots,
While eels keep secrets, connecting the dots.

At the bottom, a laugh echoes wide,
In the depths where the whispers collide.
Not just a water world, but a playful show,
Where funny is found in the ebbs and flows.

Secrets in the Tidepools

Tidepools hide laughter in craggy nooks,
Where sea slugs scribble in forgotten books.
Crabs wear sunglasses, looking so cool,
While kelp sways and plays like a jolly fool.

Starfish roll dice on the ocean floor,
While anemones dance, begging for more.
Tiny fish pirouette, a chubby ballet,
As seagulls watch on, hoping to stay.

The ocean sighs in a bubbly chatter,
With mollusks debating what truly matters.
A clam tells jokes that could crack a shell,
Leaving all friends in a giggling swell.

In pools where the sunlight does twinkle and play,
Secrets unravel in a watery way.
Each ripple carries a hint of delight,
In this rocky theater, laughter takes flight.

Rhythms of the Abyss

In the deep where fish do dance,
A crab sings songs of a tall romance.
Octopuses throw a wild soirée,
While seaweed joins in on the fray.

A clam won the limbo contest,
While starfish just take their rest.
But wait, what's that? A whale's on a spree,
Doing the cha-cha, full of glee!

Turtles try to catch a beat,
With flippers flapping, oh so sweet.
Jellyfish glow like disco balls,
As bubbles rise and laughter calls.

So come dive in, don't miss the fun,
Where mischiefs play till day is done.
Under waves where joy is found,
The rhythm of the abyss knows no bounds!

Reflections in a Teardrop

In droplets where fish tales swirl,
A minnow wears a party pearl.
Sea cucumbers snicker and peek,
At all the gossip that they speak.

A sponge in the corner, quite the tease,
Claims it can tickle the swaying breeze.
Meanwhile, a shrimp puts on a show,
With dance moves only critters know.

A turtle lost a bet to a crab,
Now wearing a shell that's just a fab.
While bubbles float like balloons in air,
Funny fish can't help but stare.

So raise a toast, with seaweed toast,
To all the creatures we love the most!
In reflections where laughter's found,
A teardrop's tale in giggles resound.

Silent Sentinels of the Tide

There stands a rock, proud and gray,
Laughing at waves that splish and play.
Barnacles gossip, clinging tight,
While crabs march by in a funny plight.

A seal balances a fish on its nose,
While dolphins tease with their acrobatic shows.
A sea urchin claims, "I'm so chic!"
As a clam throws shade—oh, how unique!

A starfish sits, plotting some pranks,
With a wink at a school of fish in ranks.
"Let's pull a stunt, let's make them shout!"
And laughter echoes, as waves toss about.

So take a moment by the shore,
Hear the silence, it's never a bore.
For sentinels, though still and wide,
Have funny tales in every tide.

Storyteller of the Waters

Once upon a wave so grand,
A fish told tales of far-off land.
With gills all flared, and fins a'flap,
It spun wild yarns, a fishy map.

An anglerfish chimed in with flair,
"Alright, alright, I'll make you stare!"
With lights aglow like disco lights,
It flashed its story, oh what sights!

A wise old turtle shook his head,
"Keep it down, or we'll wake the dead!"
But jellyfish giggled, floating near,
"When the tide is right, we'll shed a tear."

So listen close to the rippling roar,
For every wave hides a tale galore.
The waters whisper in curious ways,
With giggles and stories in endless plays.

Lullabies of the Drowned

Bubbles dance in watery tunes,
Fish wear hats, like little loons.
Octopuses clap, all in a row,
That's how the tides put on a show.

Seahorses spin on their tiny tails,
Crabs tell jokes that never fails.
With laughter echoing in the deep,
They gaze at the world, while fish doze and sleep.

Mermaids sing with a toothbrush mic,
While dolphins dance like they're on a bike.
It's a party down where the currents play,
Under the waves, it's a wacky soiree!

When bubbles burst, there's a comic flare,
And jellyfish float without a care.
In this realm where gags abound,
The comedians of the ocean are crowned!

The Invisible Hand Beneath

Waves whisper tales of fishy plight,
When starfish hang out, oh what a sight!
They play cards with shells, in a game so neat,
While sea turtles cheer from their comfy seat.

Invisible hands give crabs a push,
As they sprint to scuttle, in a hurry, a rush!
With a wink and a wave, they start to prance,
In a crabby ballet, they all take a chance.

Under swirling currents, laughter flows,
With underwater tickles that nobody knows.
A ticklish whale shakes the ground,
Causing otters to roll, oh what a sound!

Between the corals, a dance party brews,
With the ocean's rhythm, how can you lose?
So join the fun and let yourself dive,
In this hidden world, the laughter's alive!

Hidden Labyrinths of Water

In the maze where the fish like to race,
Turtles lose track in a wild chase.
Sneaky eels play hide and seek,
Poking their heads, oh so unique!

The snails on a stroll are quite the sight,
Wearing tiny caps that sparkle just right.
While sea stars map out their plans for the night,
Flipping the script, what an actual fright!

Anemones wave, like they're saying hello,
As clownfish wiggle with a fervent glow.
They giggle and tease, all in good fun,
In this watery carnival, laughing's never done.

With crabs on roller skates, it's a scene,
Where every splash seems like a dream.
In this underwater amusement park,
Joy shines through every watery arc!

Realms of the Ocean's Soul

In playful depths, where treasures gleam,
Goldfish host parties, a vibrant theme.
With disco balls crafted from shells,
They twirl and whirl, in aquatic swells.

Giant squid with a paintbrush flair,
Coloring the currents with a dazzling air.
They whip up a mural on the ocean floor,
A masterpiece where mermaids adore!

Whales tell tall tales with a hearty laugh,
Exaggerating size, like a king-sized calf.
And with every splash, the waves applaud,
In this realm where humor's the main facade.

So let's dive down, where the jokes flow free,
In the hidden waters, come swim with me!
With fishy delights and snickers galore,
The realm of giggles, who could ask for more?

The Ocean's Secret Sanctuary

In the depths where seaweed twirls,
Fish gossip like excited girls.
They share tales of lost flip-flops,
And how the tide always stops.

Shells wear hats made of coral lace,
Jellyfish dance in a wobbly race.
Crabs hold court with a pincer snap,
While starfish lounge, taking a nap.

Sand dollars play the luck game right,
Wishing on stars that glow at night.
The currents hum a silly tune,
As seagulls laugh beneath the moon.

Turtles argue about who's the best,
In a lazy contest of who can rest.
And dolphins leap with a splash of glee,
In this wacky sea jubilee!

Timeless Currents

Waves roll in, the surfboard's thrill,
Tides chase each other, what a skill.
The ocean's chess with a checkered wave,
Who knew water could be so brave?

Seagulls squawk like they've lost their way,
While fish play tag in a sea ballet.
An octopus shows off its cool,
Doing more tricks than you learned in school.

The tide's a joker, always late,
Making sandcastles that can't quite wait.
Mermaids giggle as they comb their hair,
While crabs throw parties without a care.

With every splash, a chuckle is found,
Within these waves, joy knows no bound.
For in these rhythms, laughter flows free,
In the currents of life's jubilee!

Footprints in the Sand of Memory

Footprints dance in the golden glow,
While seagulls scratch a silly show.
Sand castles guard forgotten dreams,
With moats that flow in silly streams.

Flip-flops lost on the ocean's breeze,
Turned into boomerangs with ease.
Kids chase waves that giggle and run,
While crabs wear shells like hats of fun.

Wet dog shakes leave splatters on pants,
As waves tease shore in merry prance.
A beach ball soars, then flops and lands,
In the hands of laughing, four-foot bands.

Memories mingle where footprints fade,
In the laughter shared, joy never traded.
What tales these shores could surely tell,
Of footprints and fun, oh so swell!

Breezes of the Hidden Depths

Breezes whisper from the ocean's floor,
With secrets only shells adore.
Crabs wear capes, heroes of stealth,
Jellyfish float with no need for wealth.

Seashells chat like old friends do,
While fish in tuxedos swim right through.
A sea cucumber in a slow-motion race,
Declares itself king, oh what a grace!

Waves tickle toes on sandy shores,
As barnacles argue with open jaws.
In this realm where laughter's a must,
Even the barnacle knows to trust!

In the hidden depths, fun reigns supreme,
As bubbles giggle and surfboards gleam.
Discovering treasures with every breeze,
These are the secrets that bring us glee!

Siren's Lament in the Coral Garden

In a garden where fish play peek-a-boo,
A siren sang tunes that were quite askew.
She danced with the crabs, quite out of her mind,
While the seaweed wiggled, leaving truth blind.

An octopus joined with eight flailing arms,
Claiming he knew all the fanciest charms.
But bubbles would burst from their laughter so loud,
Even the starfish thought they were quite proud.

The clownfish rolled eyes at the comedic scene,
As dolphins would giggle, their laughter routine.
"Why not a conga?" the seahorse did plead,
"Let's dance in the currents, and fulfill this need!"

But the siren just chuckled, "Oh, isn't it grand?
To have friends in this watery, whimsical land!"
So they twirled and they whirled with no hint of a care,
In the coral garden, joy filled the air!

Submerged Stories of Time

Down where the bubbles hold secrets untold,
The fish share their stories, both silly and bold.
A clam dropped a pearl that fell from his shell,
"I'd trade it for laughter, I'm under this spell!"

The turtles recounted their races so slow,
"Bet you can't catch me!" said a bright yellow glow.
While eels slipped and slithered, all tangled in glee,
"Someone call a diver! This mess isn't me!"

A wise old conch gave his best advice:
"Laugh at your troubles, they pay off quite nice!"
The gulls wheeled above, with quips of their own,
As waves rolled by singing their seaweed tone.

So somewhere ensconced in the deep azure lore,
Are stories of silliness waiting to soar.
With every new ripple, each wave that aligns,
Lives laughter and joy in these buoyant designs!

Symphony of the Forgotten Waves

The waves formed a band, if you listened real close,
Each splash was a note, like a raucous old ghost.
With seafoam for violins, clams played the drums,
And all of the fish joined, singing tales of their chums.

They tuned to the rhythm of a wobbly tide,
With dolphins in tutus, adorned and dignified.
A jellyfish glowed, in disco delight,
Making moves on the sand as if they were right!

The sea turtles nodded, keeping slow beats,
While mermaids beamed proudly in sparkly seats.
But a stormy old whale puffed in with a roar,
"Don't make me a backup!" he announced with a snore.

Yet laughter erupted, a chorus so sweet,
As the waves swirled in tune, on this strange, salty street.
So here in the depths, a performance unfolds,
In laughter and waves, fun in stories retold!

Thalassic Whispers of Solitude

In the depths of the blue, where few dare to roam,
A starfish looked out, dreaming of home.
With each gentle wave, he whispered his wish,
"I'd trade for some fun, maybe a fishy dish!"

A crab overheard him and said with a wink,
"Join us for shenanigans, come take a drink!"
They sipped on seaweed and played card games sly,
While seagulls above let out raucous cries.

An eel slid on in with a wink and a smile,
"I thought I'd stop by and make life worthwhile!"
The jellyfish giggled, glow lighting the scene,
"Solitude's nice, but it's better with a team!"

So they laughed, and they played in their watery dome,
Casting aside dreariness far from their home.
In the whispers of waves, they found gleeful delight,
A buoyant reminder that joy takes its flight!

Secrets of the Salted Wind

A crab once wore a jaunty hat,
It danced and pranced, imagine that!
He claimed to be a noble lord,
But crabs just scuttle, how absurd!

The seagulls squawked, 'What's the fuss?'
They knocked his hat and made a fuss.
With all their squawking in the breeze,
That crab, he turned with utmost ease!

A fish in school said, "What a sight!"
"Does he think he's in a royal fight?"
The waves just chuckled, rolling fast,
As crab's great dreams were left in past.

So if you see a crab with flair,
Just laugh with joy, don't you dare stare.
For in the surf, the truth's so clear,
It's just a crab—no lords here, dear!

Myths of the Moonlit Waves

A dolphin tried to serenade,
With tunes so wild, we'd all cascade!
But what emerged, oh what a sound,
The fish all flopped, spun round and round!

The starfish giggled on the floor,
"Is that a tune or seaweed's snore?"
The moonlit night began to sway,
With laughter echoing, come what may!

A clam proclaimed, "No more, I plead!"
"Your voice is worse than seaweed's greed!"
But dolphin danced with reckless cheer,
As fish just swam away in fear!

At dawn, they said, "What a delight!"
"Let's leave the tunes for moonlit nights!"
And in the waves, they shared a glance,
For fluffy dolphins just love to dance!

Underbelly of the Deep

Down in the depths, where jellyfish glow,
An octopus tries to put on a show.
He juggled fish with eight-armed flair,
But oh, the fish just didn't care!

A shrimp yelled out, "What skill you've got!"
But all the fish just swam on the spot.
"Would you prefer a game of tag?"
And before they knew it, the fish were wag!

The fish swirled round, with speed and glee,
While octopus sighed in misery.
"Next time I'll try a magic trick,
Something that won't make 'em sick!"

So if you dive to that tricky place,
Remember the octopus's grace.
He may be clumsy, but with a heart,
He's still the one who plays the part!

Melodies of the Deep Blue

A fish with a hat danced at dawn,
It played a trombone, the sea's own fawn.
Crabs clapped along with a pinch and a grin,
While octopuses jived with eight-legged spin.

Starfish formed a band on a rock,
With coral trumpets, they started to talk.
A dolphin DJ scratched the waves just right,
As everyone grooved, what a glorious sight!

Turtles in shades were the coolest of all,
They rolled up their fins, ready for the ball.
Underwater disco, a bubblegum spree,
The ocean's a party, oh won't you agree?

When the sun dipped low, "Let's kayak!" they cheered,
But whales in tuxedos had all disappeared.
So they settled down for a fishy buffet,
With laughter and joy in their own special way.

Celestial Waters

Mermaids hold meetings with glittering eyes,
Debating the best place to hide their pies.
They giggle and whisper, tales of old,
Of crumpets and crabs, and treasures all told.

Seahorses zoomed in tiny parade,
While sea urchins plotted a cunning charade.
"Let's steal a sea cucumber!" someone shouted,
And laughter erupted, no one was doubted.

A whale on a surfboard tried tricks with a flip,
But ended up splashing with a comical slip.
Clownfish rolled over, their stripes out of sync,
As oysters discussed the next big shell drink.

At dusk they all gathered, exchanged silly jokes,
While jellyfish floated like graceful folks.
In this watery realm, with giggles galore,
The antics unfold, who could ask for more?

Journey to the Ocean Floor

Down, down we dove, past seaweed and light,
Where clams argued loudly, and eels took flight.
Anemones danced as we stumbled and spun,
While barnacles cheered, "Join in the fun!"

A crab with a cape shouted, "Follow me!"
As we snickered and snorkeled, what sights did we see?
A clam wearing glasses, a fish with a phone,
It's true what they say, the deep's never alone.

Octopuses traded their best favorite snacks,
While shrimp built sandcastles, with beach towel packs.
The journey was wild, so much to adore,
Underwater hijinks, we couldn't ignore.

But as we swam up, there was giggling galore,
Tangled in bubbles, we burst out with roar.
The ocean's a circus, with laughter and cheer,
Who knew deep down was so fun, oh dear?

Treasures of the Abyss

In the depths where the shadows play tricks on the eyes,
A dueling squid made some kooky guys rise.
With treasure chests full of mismatched old toys,
They plotted to play pranks, oh what silly joys.

A turtleneck turtle wore stripes just for flair,
While jellyfish pranced without a single care.
"Find me a crown made of seaweeds and shells!"
Cried a crab king who rang all the underwater bells.

The laughter echoed through caverns so wide,
Where sea cucumbers rolled, googly-eyed.
They found ancient coins that were really just gum,
And they laughed at the thought, what a silly sum!

The treasures they found were not diamonds or gold,
But friendships and giggles, bright tales to be told.
So in this deep world, where the waters may twist,
Every creature knows laughter is the best treasure list!

Sunken Souls and Salty Tears

In the depths where fish do hide,
A crab once wore a pirate's pride.
He danced around with clumsy glee,
Saying, 'Look at me! I'm a treasure, you see!'

Floating bottles, messages cry,
'Help! I lost my sandwich!' oh my!
The jellyfish, they giggle and sway,
In this salty ballet, they play all day.

A dolphin sings a tune so sweet,
While seagulls steal the fries we eat.
Underwater, the antics are grand,
With a clam which claims to be in a band!

So if you hear a splash and a cheer,
It's likely a fish that found a beer.
Just remember, with every wave,
Laughter is what the ocean gave!

The Ocean's Veiled Embrace

With barnacles stuck on a wooden boat,
A whale tried swimming, but missed the note.
He serenades with a voice so deep,
While sea turtles join in, a rhythmic sweep.

Octopuses juggle with great finesse,
While sea urchins shout, 'Well, that's a mess!'
A starfish flips, looking quite grand,
Claiming he's king of the beach sand land.

The tide rolls in, and clams complain,
'Why do we always get all this rain?'
But crabs, they dance, never feeling down,
In their crustacean capers, wearing a crown.

So when you dip your toes in the foam,
Just know that creatures are never alone.
Down below, fun bubbles and cheers,
In this watery world, humor appears!

Mysteries Wrapped in Waves

A mermaid sits on a rock so fine,
Wishing for popcorn and a nice glass of wine.
She waves to sailors but gets a frown,
They think she's just trying to lure them down.

An octopus plays hide and seek,
With fish that giggle and hide when they peek.
Seashells gossip about the sun,
'Can you believe that shrimp? He's always on the run!'

When barnacles hold their grand parade,
Starfish wear hats, feeling quite made.
A grumpy old flounder shouts from afar,
'Is this party just for fish, or is it for all?'

So jump in the waves, let your worries float,
Join the dance of the rocks and the boat.
For under the surface, where giggles reside,
Laughter is endless, with friends by your side!

Deep Currents of Longing

In the depths where the seashells twirl,
A seahorse daydreams, caught in a whirl.
He wishes for tacos, not just for moss,
While searching for flavors, feeling the loss.

Fish sing songs about old shipwrecks,
While buried treasures give them the heck.
Mysteries swirl in bubbles and foam,
As crabs make their way to a fancy new home.

A narwhal jokes, 'I've got a long horn,
Perfect for poking at ice cream, oh warn!'
Turtles chuckle, still playing their games,
While seagulls steal fries and shout out their names.

So dive in and splash, let your joy be free,
For underwater antics are meant to be!
With laughter it glimmers, like sun on the deep,
In the currents of longing, fun secrets we keep!

Cradled by the Celestial Deep

A fish in a tux, what a sight!
He dances and twirls under the moonlight.
With bubbles for ties and laughter so loud,
He sways with the kelp, a delighted crowd.

Starfish snapping selfies, oh what a pose!
An octopus artist in watercolors shows.
They paint with the tides and glimmering gold,
These slippery dreams can never grow old.

Coral reefs giggle, what a ruckus they make,
As clams tell their tales of the wonders at stake.
Driftwood turns storyteller, woven in lore,
While crabs hold the stage, giving comedy more.

Each wave carries secrets, a burst of delight,
Playing hide and seek under the stars so bright.
In this merry realm, joy dances and swirls,
Life's a splashy joke for all the sea-worlds!

The Treasure of Fathomless Dreams

A treasure map drawn by a curious shrimp,
Leading to giggles, not gold nor a blimp.
X marks a spot where the turtles dive deep,
In search of lost socks, or so the tales creep.

Pufferfish puckered, they float like balloons,
Belly laughs echo in whimsical tunes.
As jellyfish jive, tentacles sway,
Mermaids join in for a sweet ballet.

Sea urchins giggle with prickle and poke,
Chasing the currents, they're the real folk.
A conch shell came in, waving a fee,
For a dance-off with seahorses, oh what glee!

With each salty wave, mischief awaits,
Dolphins who prank have the best of fates.
In this sunlit cove, laughter's the prize,
Finding joy in the depths, oh, what a surprise!

Brine and Bone: An Unseen Tale

In waters where whispers of bones make a show,
Skeletons glide, putting on quite the glow.
They host midnight feasts, what a spooky delight,
As seaweed serves snacks beneath the moonlight.

Mermaids marvel at cloths made from eels,
Knitting with scales that boast quirky appeals.
Beware of the winks from the shark that's quite sly,
He's planning a party, you're all invited—oh my!

With crabs in tuxedos and clams dressed to thrill,
The underwater gala, come see if you will.
Bubbles for drinks, floating pearls for the toast,
A jester fish juggling will make you laugh most!

But watch out for narwhals, jesters of lore,
They tell all the tales, and then ask for more.
As night fades away and the sun starts to yawn,
Secrets still linger, but jesters are gone!

Luminescent Secrets of the Ocean Floor

Glow worms and lanternfish twinkle at night,
While wonders unfold, all full of delight.
Dancing amidst currents, an electric parade,
With laughter like bubbles, no need for charade.

A crab in a hat does the cha-cha with flair,
Bubbles pop like popcorn, joy fills the air.
The sea cucumber giggles, all squishy and bright,
He says, 'I'm a veggie, just basking in light!'

A lost underwater sock gets a standing ovation,
As jellyfish groove with wild fascination.
Each wave breaks a punchline, a slapstick affair,
In this glowing abyss, humor's beyond compare.

As tides pull the jokes from the depths of the swell,
Creatures unite with tales they don't tell.
This world full of wonders, of giggles and cheer,
Hides laughter at depths where no one will hear!

Reefside Reflections

A crab in a tuxedo, struts down the sand,
He claims he's the king, ruling this land.
A fish in a top hat, gives him a wink,
Together they laugh, over a drink.

The octopus juggles, with style and grace,
But trips on a starfish, what a strange place!
The seaweed giggles, this lively affair,
As bubbles float up, swirling in air.

A conch shell conducts, a band of old tunes,
While shrimp dance around, under bright, glowing moons.

Clownfish in costumes, tease the poor snails,
As dolphins whistle, telling tall tales.

In this underwater party, all is so bright,
With laughter and joy, from morning till night.
So grab your snorkel and join in the fun,
For reefside reflections have only begun!

Shimmering Depths of Fate

A mermaid lost socks, oh what a sight,
She's searching high and low, from morning to night.
An angelfish giggles, with a sparkle in eye,
'Those socks won't return, so don't even try!'

A turtle slow dances, with coral as his date,
Both wobble and swirl, it's a marvelous fate.
The seahorses chuckle, at the clumsy old pair,
While nudibranchs skate, with glittering flair.

A pirate's old parrot, gets lost on a quest,
For treasure, he thinks, but he only found jest.
He squawks tales of daring, of far-away gold,
But it's just stinky seaweed, or so I am told!

In these shimmering depths, laughter reigns supreme,
Where every old creature has fun in their dream.
So dive in, my friend, give your worries a break,
And dance with the fish in this colorful lake!

Beneath the Surface

Beneath the blue waves, where fish wear a bow,
A lobster runs for mayor, with quite the show.
He promises all shrimp, a life full of fun,
But they laugh and they say, 'He's only a pun!'

A seagull's got jokes, as he flies overhead,
With puns about krill, that he claims he once fed.
The flounders roll their eyes, in their flat little way,
As they flip and they flop, in a laid-back display.

A dolphin in glasses, reads stories of lore,
To fish gathered 'round, hoping for more.
With tales of a treasure, buried long ago,
It turns out to be clams, how silly, you know!

Here beneath the surface, life is a giggle,
Every bubble that rises, makes us all wiggle.
So swim with the currents, let laughter unleash,
In this playful abyss, there's joy as a feast!

Anemone Dreams

In anemones cozy, the clownfish reside,
Playing hide and seek, oh what a fun ride!
With tickles from tentacles, they giggle and squeal,
As jellyfish sway, like a wobbly wheel.

A shrimp with a trumpet, starts up the band,
But the sea cucumber hoots, 'That's not how it's planned!'

Shells start to dance, to the funky old beat,
As barnacles tap-tap, to the rhythm so sweet.

A dolphin groans loudly, with a face of dismay,
'This music's a ruckus, please take it away!'
But all of the critters just bellyache loud,
Claiming that chaos brings joy to the crowd!

In these anemone dreams, where laughter takes flight,
Each creature's a star, twinkling under the night.
So let's party forever, without any schemes,
For here in these waters, it's all about dreams!

The Wise Ones of the Brine

In the depths where the laughter flows,
The fish wear glasses, striking a pose.
They gossip 'bout crabs in two-piece suits,
And debate what's best: seaweed or roots.

The jellyfish dance with elegant grace,
While the octopus makes a silly face.
They tell tall tales of sailors' misdeeds,
And whisper sweet nothings to wandering reeds.

Anemones host a bizarre comedy,
While turtles judge with utmost glee.
They crack jokes about deep-water woes,
As clams clap shells, and the whole party grows.

With bubbles of laughter that rise and pop,
The wise ones of brine never want to stop.
They toast to the waves, with a wink and a cheer,
For in salty depths, fun is always near.

Wind-Swept Chronicles

With each breeze that tickles the sail,
The waves tell stories, without fail.
Of mischievous dolphins, playing with foam,
And seagulls stealing lunch to take home.

The sailboats giggle as they tip and slide,
While pirates argue about their pride.
'Yo ho ho!' they bellow with glee,
While a crab rolls his eyes, sipping his tea.

Mermaids gossip while combing their hair,
Swapping old tales with a touch of flair.
'The tide brought me treasure, or so I thought!'
Now it's just a shoe—oh, the battles fought!

A plankton parade dances with zest,
As windswept chroniclers take a rest.
With laughter and tales that boldly expand,
The chronicles blow through this whimsical land.

Lost Hopes in the Coral Chambré

In a coral room where dreams take a dive,
A fish lost his keys, but he still feels alive.
He trips on a starfish, spills jellybeans wide,
And grumbles aloud, 'Can I just take a ride?'

The clam's a collector of old, shiny junk,
While mermaids trade secrets with pirates who funk.
With laughter, they sift through sunken treasure,
Finding lost hopes that shimmer with pleasure.

A message in a bottle floats by with a shout,
'Help! I'm a sandwich! Please pull me out!'
But the salmon just chuckles, 'You're quite misplaced,
I'll take you to brine, there's no time to waste!'

In the coral chambré, where silliness reigns,
Hopes swim around in buoyant chains.
With each laughter and jest, they spin and twine,
Lost dreams in a habitat both quirky and fine.

Kaleidoscope of Tidal Stories

Under the waves, a tale unfolds,
Where crabs stack stories like towers of gold.
The shells listen close to every tall tale,
While fish flash their colors, a whimsical trail.

A dolphin declares, 'I'll be the historian!
My memory's sharp; don't call me a historian!'
He winks at a starfish, both clueless they seem,
As they spin every story into a dream.

Turtles move slow, but think fast, oh dear!
'Is it Tuesday or Friday?' they scratch at their ear.
They reminisce quickly of dandy ship sails,
While the plankton cue up, singing sea tales.

A kaleidoscope twirls with each splash and chime,
A silliness echoing through sea's quaint rhyme.
For in every wave, a new giggle can start,
With legends of depth that tickle the heart.

Aquatic Whispers of Eternity

Fish in tuxedos, having a ball,
Tangoing under the ocean's great hall.
Jellybeans waltz with a splash and a grin,
While crabs don top hats and spin with a spin.

Octopuses juggling bright seashells with flair,
Sea turtles take selfies, with scales nice and bare.
Anemones giggle, as clams hum a tune,
The sea's a big party, from sunrise to moon.

Mermaids serve cocktails, with bubbles galore,
Shaking their tails, they dance on the floor.
Dolphins are knights, jousting with foam,
In this underwater play, everyone's home.

So dive in for laughter, forget all your woes,
Join sea critters laughing, where fun always flows.
Bubbles of joy rise, tickling the tide,
In this lively realm, where hilarity's wide.

Rippling Reveries

Seahorses prancing in frothy ballet,
With anemones cheering, 'Hip-hip-hooray!'
Starfish do yoga on rocks in a line,
While squids sketch portraits with ink that's divine.

Walruses wear glasses, reading the news,
While crabs play charades in their funny shoes.
Turtles trade gossip as they take a stroll,
With bubbles of laughter that roll and unroll.

A pufferfish grins, 'Just puffed up today!'
Yoga classes fill up, it's quite the display.
Tides tickle the beaches, join in the fun,
This whimsical world is where jokes are spun.

So catch a good wave, let your worries drift,
In this charming ocean, where giggles are gift.
With every splash and ripple, join in the cheer,
For underwater laughter is always near.

Undercurrents of Time

Clownfish cracking jokes, don't take things too slow,
With seaweeds as curtains for their comedy show.
Barnacles chuckle while glued to their rocks,
While dolphins keep score with their sleek silver clocks.

Time seems to giggle, as waves ebb and flow,
A hula-hooping lobster, ready to go!
Shrimp throwing parties, inviting the crew,
With a confetti of bubbles, each pop's something new.

Those grumpy old cods can't stop rolling their eyes,
As the young fish parade in their shiny disguise.
Time makes a joke, 'I'm always behind!'
In this silly sea, laughter's easily mined.

So let's dive into dreams where humor is prime,
In waters where whimsy dances through time.
Every splash tells a tale with a twist and a turn,
In this aquatic circus, there's always a learn.

Light and Shadow Beneath the Waves

Beneath the blue waves, where shadows can play,
Squid are the artists in a grand cabaret.
With colors that dance, and shapes that surprise,
They giggle in laughter, under saltwater skies.

Cowardly crabs hide in shells just to peep,
While dolphins spin tales in the currents so deep.
Flashlight fish flicker, creating a show,
Lighting up dark spaces, where laughter can grow.

Whales make a ruckus with songs from the heart,
While seahorses spin, doing their ballet art.
Shadows take shape, like imaginations run wild,
In the ocean's embrace, each creature is a child.

Let's treasure these moments, these giggles we find,
In the depths of the ocean, where all's intertwined.
With laughter and joy, lifting spirits to soar,
In this vibrant abyss, we're never a bore.

www.ingramcontent.com/pod-product-compliance
Lightning Source LLC
Chambersburg PA
CBHW060142230426
43661CB00003B/536